Super Sea Creatures



# OCTOPUSES

GAIL TERP

BLACK RABBIT BOOKS

Bolt is published by Black Rabbit Books
P.O. Box 3263, Mankato, Minnesota, 56002.
www.blackrabbitbooks.com


Marysa Storm, editor; Grant Gould, designer;
Omay Ayres, photo researcher



Names: Terp, Gail, 1951- author.
Title: Octopuses / by Gail Terp.
Description: Mankato, Minnesota : Black Rabbit Books, [2021] | Series: Bolt. super sea creatures | Includes bibliographical references and index. | Audience: Ages 8-12 | Audience: Grades 4-6 | Summary: "Dive into learning about octopuses with vibrant photography, engaging text, and range maps, size comparisons, and other infographics"- Provided by publisher. Identifiers: LCCN 2019026681 (print) | LCCN 2019026682 (ebook) | ISBN 9781623102838 (hardcover) | ISBN 9781644663790 (paperback) | ISBN 9781623103774 (ebook)
Subjects: LCSH: Octopuses–Juvenile literature.
Classification: LCC QL430.3.O2 T45 2021 (print) | LCC QL430.3.O2 (ebook) | DDC 594/.56-dc23
LC record available at https://lccn.loc.gov/2019026681
LC ebook record available at https://lccn.loc.gov/2019026682

Printed in the United States. 2/20

## Image Credits

Alamy: BIOSPHOTO, 32; blickwinkel, Cover; BluePlanetArchive: Martin Strmiska, 4–5, 14; Dreamstime: Fiona Ayerst, 15 (btm); Minden: Alex Mustard, 27; Fred Bavendam, 18 (btm); Shinji Kusano, 21 (btm); Yasumasa Kobayashi, 22; festo.com: Festo, 28 (btm); iStock: protog, 6; mauimagazine.net: Maui Magazine, 8–9; Science Source: Jeff Rotman, 12; Shutterstock: Alexey Masliy, 15 (top); Andi de Boer, 3; ArtMari, 16–17 (silhouettes); Channarong Pherngjanda, 16–17 (bkgd); divedog, 18 (top); Evlakhov Valeriy, 24 (eel); Fotokon, 28 (top); fototrips, 24 (crab); Guitar photographer, 24 (lobster); Konstantin G, 24 (whale); Moon_Raiter, 24 (fish); pan demin, 1, 10–11; pr2is, 22–23; Stasis Photo, 31; Tao Jiang, 24 (bird); Yellow Cat, 24 (octopus); twitter.com: Ocean Gate, 21 (top)

# CONTENTS

CHAPTER 1

# IN THE SEA

A crab crawls along the ocean floor. An octopus is close by. But the crab doesn't see it. The octopus has changed its color. It looks just like the rocks and sand around it. Suddenly, the octopus grabs the crab and brings it close. The octopus uses its beak to make a hole in the crab's shell. It then scrapes out the meat. Dinnertime!

## COMPARING LENGTHS

## Blending In

About 300 kinds of octopus swim in the oceans. These animals use camouflage to hide. Their skin changes color to match their surroundings. Octopuses can hide by changing shapes too. They have no bones and can stretch to look like plants. They can ball up to look like rocks.

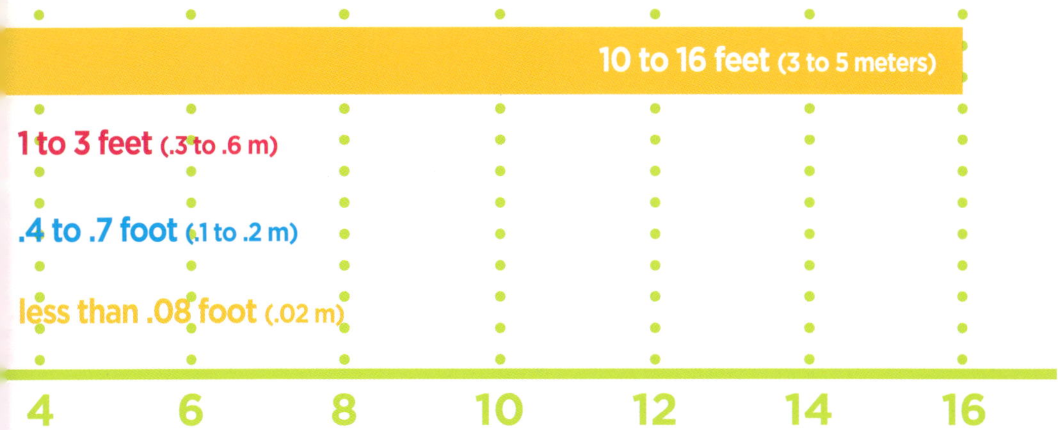

## Many Arms

Octopuses are smart animals with great eyesight. They all have eight arms. Each arm is covered with two rows of suckers. The suckers have chemical **receptors**. These help octopuses taste whatever they touch.

Octopuses use their arms and suckers all the time. They use them to explore the ocean floor. They also use them to find and grab **prey**.

Octopuses can travel in many different ways. They can crawl on the ocean floor or swim. For quick travel, they propel themselves by shooting water from their bodies.

# OCTOPUS FEATURES

BEAK
(LOCATED UNDER BODY)
SUCKERS

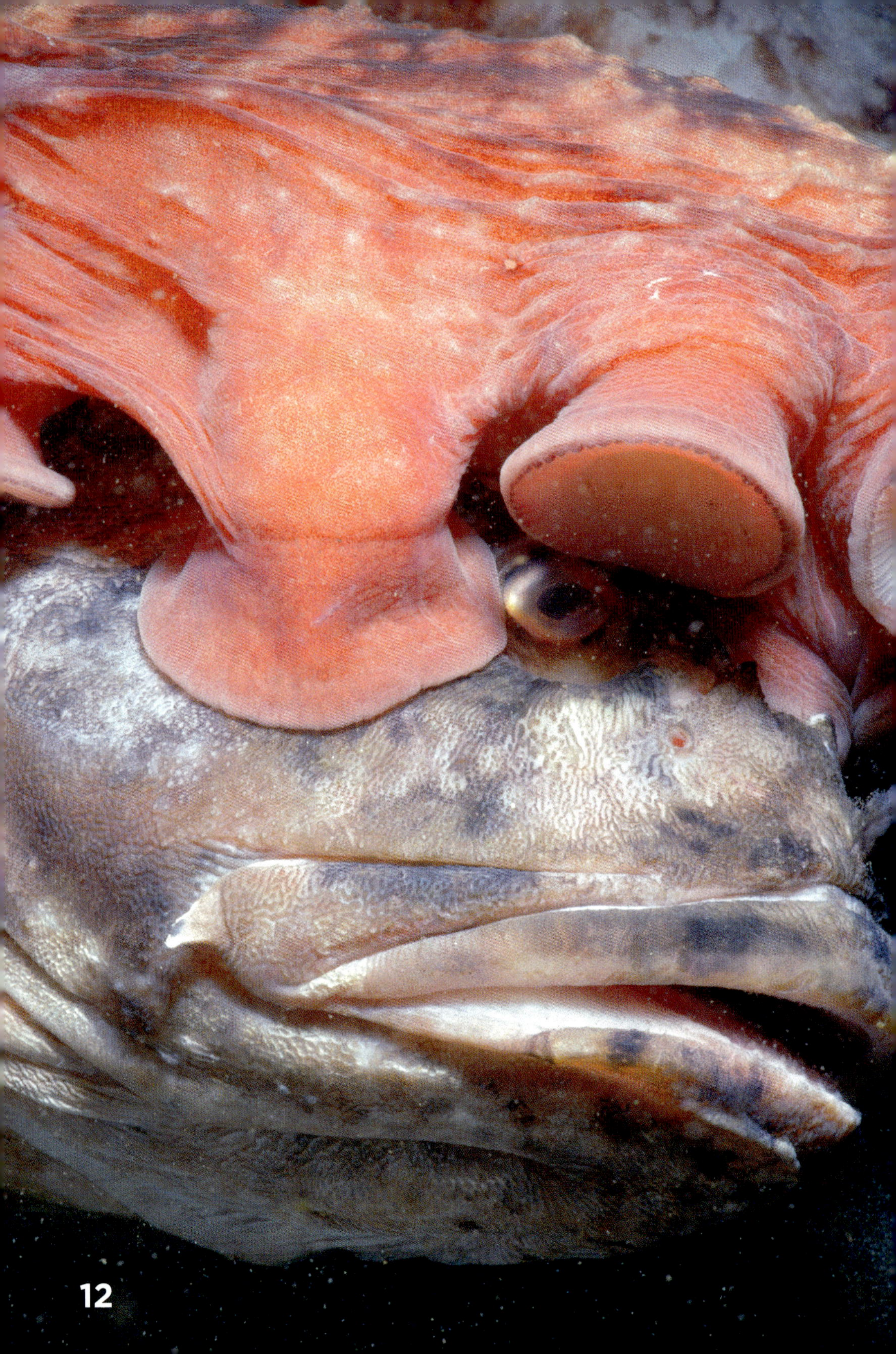

# CHAPTER 2

# FOOD TO EAT and a Place to Live

Octopuses eat many different things. They sometimes eat fish. Large octopuses can eat sharks. Some also eat other octopuses. They mostly eat crustaceans, such as lobsters and crabs, though. They often break the shells with their beaks.

**Octopuses have blue blood.**

## Habitats

Octopuses live in oceans all over the world. They spend most of their time on ocean floors. Many live near coral reefs.

An octopus lives alone in a den. The size of the den depends on the size of the octopus. Most octopuses change homes often.

# Where Octopuses Make Dens

caves and rocks

shells

coral reefs

# WHERE OCTOPUSES LIVE

## Octopus Range Map

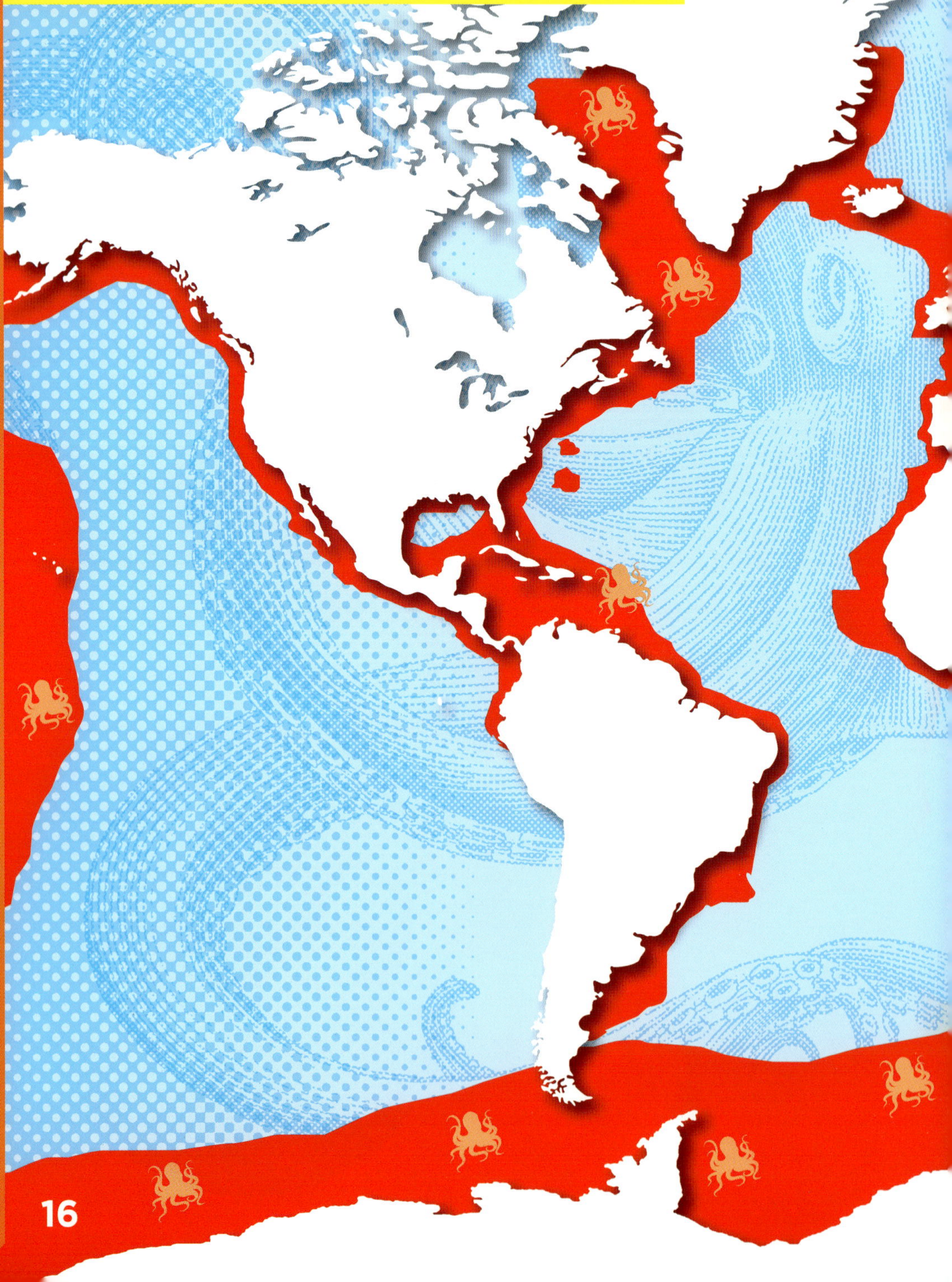

# CHAPTER 3

# FAMILY LIFE

Octopuses meet to **mate**. They only mate once in their life. After mating, females release many eggs into the water. The mothers stay with the eggs. They don't even leave to eat. They spend all their time guarding the eggs. **Predators**, such as fish, would love to gobble them up.

**Males and females can be different sizes. A female blanket octopus can be almost 100 times bigger than a male.**

## Time to Hatch

After at least a month, octopus eggs hatch. Some types hatch as full octopuses. Others hatch as **larvae**. The larvae simply float in the ocean for a month or more. They grow into octopuses. Octopus parents don't take care of the babies. The young are on their own.

**There's a reason octopuses only mate once. Males die after mating. Sometimes the females eat them. Shortly after the eggs hatch, the females die.**

HATCHLING

LARVAE

# BY THE NUMBERS

**18,000 TO MORE THAN 200,000**

NUMBER OF EGGS A FEMALE RELEASES

**up to 6 years**

LIFE SPAN

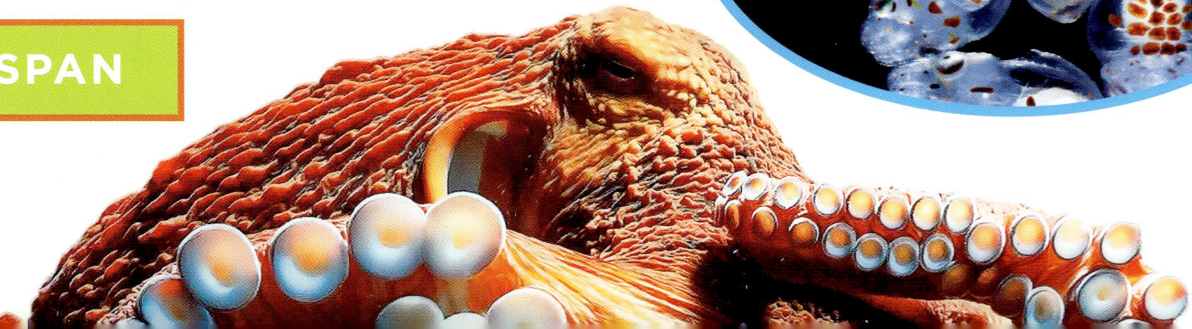

3
NUMBER OF HEARTS EACH OCTOPUS HAS
more than 600 pounds
(272 kilograms)
WEIGHT OF HEAVIEST RECORDED GIANT PACIFIC OCTOPUS

# Octopus Food Chain

This food chain shows what eats octopuses. It also shows what octopuses eat.

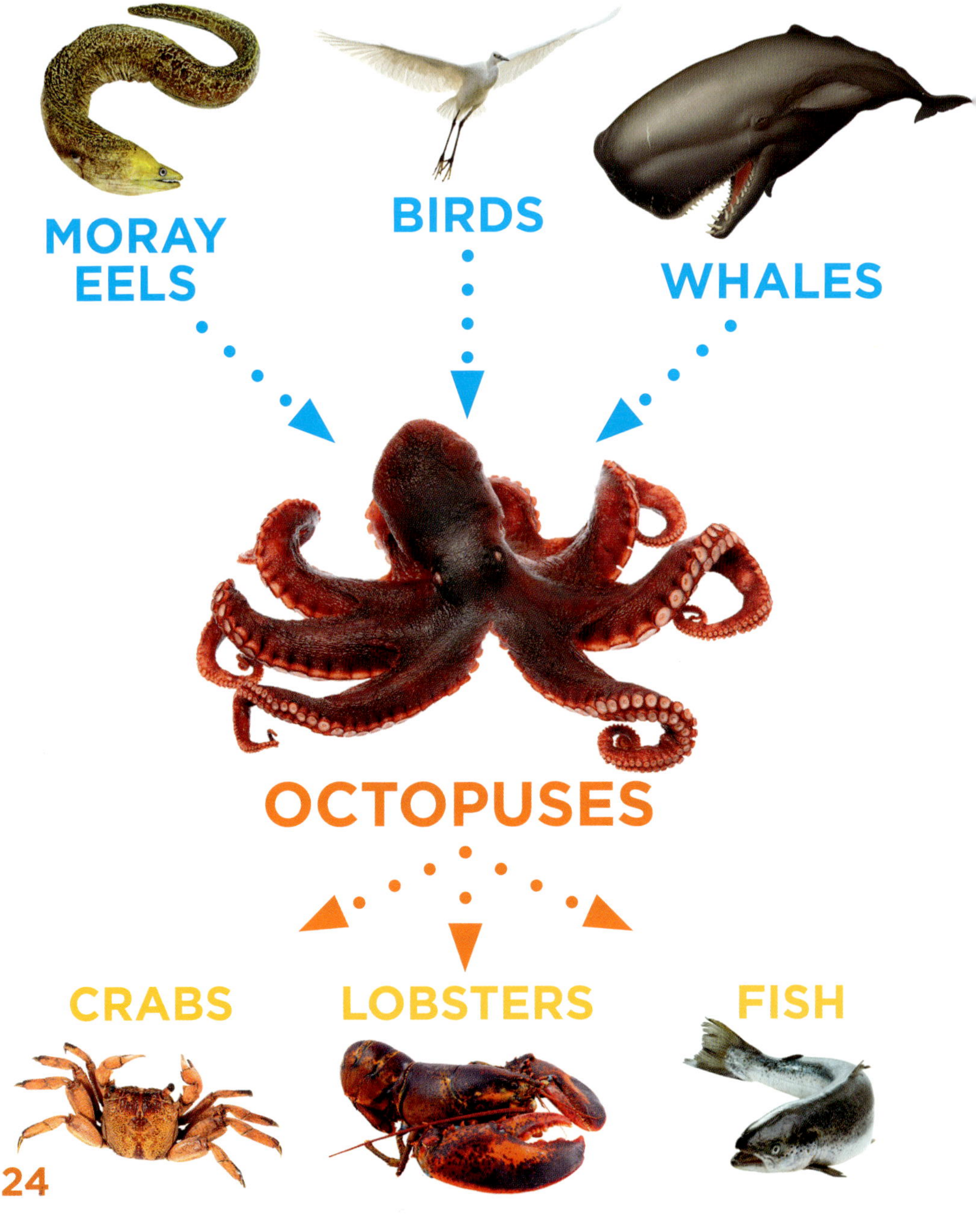

# CHAPTER 4

# Part of THEIR WORLD

Octopuses have predators. Fish, birds, and moray eels eat them. Large animals, such as whales and seals, eat them too.

Octopuses aren't easy to hunt, though. They have ways to stay safe. Octopuses can shoot out black ink. The ink confuses predators, and octopuses can escape. Some change their shapes to look like deadly animals. Enemies back off. An octopus will even let a predator take one of its arms. It can regrow the arm later.

## Human Threats

Octopuses face dangers from humans too. Humans hunt octopuses for food. Some octopus populations are shrinking because too many are killed.

Human actions affect octopus habitats too. **Global warming** and **pollution** hurt coral reefs. The reefs aren't as healthy. Octopuses have fewer places to live. They have less food to hunt.

Octopuses help scientists. Scientists study the animals to learn how to make better robots. New robots might use suckers to grab things.

## Protecting Octopuses

Octopuses are an important part of their **ecosystems**. Humans need to protect octopuses and their habitats. These creatures provide food for some animals. They eat other animals too. These smart animals truly are super sea creatures.

**ecosystem** (E-co-sys-tum)—a community of living things in one place

**global warming** (GLO-buhl WARM-ing)—a warming of Earth's air and oceans

**larva** (LAR-vuh)—the wormlike form of an animal after hatching from an egg

**mate** (MAYT)—to join together to produce young

**pollution** (puh-LOO-shun)—substances that make land, water, or air dirty and not safe to use

**predator** (PRED-uh-tuhr)—an animal that eats other animals

**prey** (PRAY)—an animal hunted or killed for food

**propel** (pruh-PEL)—to push someone or something forward or in a particular direction

**receptor** (ree-SEP-tuhr)—a nerve ending that senses changes in light, temperature, pressure, or other things and causes the body to react to it

## BOOKS

**Grunbaum, Mara.** *Octopuses: Clever Ocean Creatures.* Nature's Children. New York: Children's Press, an imprint of Scholastic Inc., 2020.

**LaPlante, Walter.** *Octopuses.* Ocean Animals. New York: Gareth Stevens Publishing, 2020.

**Meister, Cari.** *Do You Really Want to Meet an Octopus?* Do You Really Want to Meet ... ? Mankato, MN: Amicus, 2019.

## WEBSITES

Fun Octopus Facts for Kids
**www.sciencekids.co.nz/sciencefacts/animals/octopus.html**

Octopus
**a-z-animals.com/animals/octopus**

Octopus
**kids.nationalgeographic.com/animals/octopus/#octopus.jpg**

# INDEX



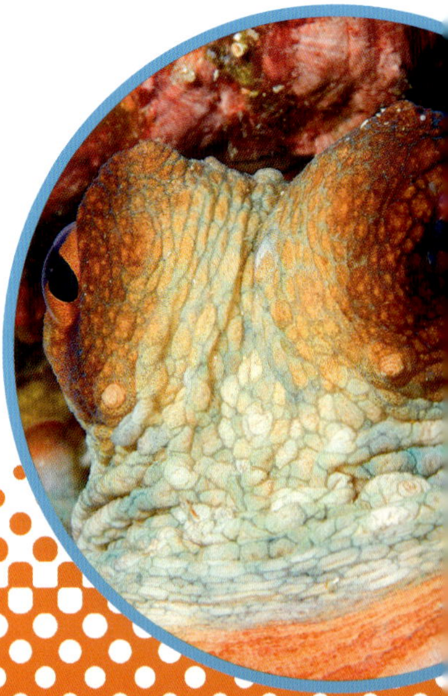